MONDAY TO FRIDAY

MONDAY TO FRIDAY

SHUBHAM KHURANA

SIMON &
SCHUSTER

London · New York · Sydney · Toronto · New Delhi

First published in India by Simon & Schuster India, 2024

1 3 5 7 9 10 8 6 4 2

Simon & Schuster India
818, Indraprakash Building,
21, Barakhamba Road,
New Delhi 110001.

www.simonandschuster.co.in

Simon & Schuster: Celebrating 100 Years of Publishing in 2024

Paperback ISBN: 978-81-970426-1-4

Typeset by Shubham Khurana
Printed and bound in India by Replika Press Pvt. Ltd.

What is Corporat Comics?

Comics about you. That's the short answer.

Corporat Comics, inspired by the proverbial corporate rat race, came to life when Shubham, a marketer by day and an undercover artist by night decided to combine his passion for sketching with the humdrum and inaneness of corporate life. The comics, sometimes hard-hitting and always sarcastic, have brought together a community of over 200,000 Corporats across the country who are not shy to laugh at themselves a little. With over 13 years as a Corporat himself, and counting, the corporate world hasn't ceased to amuse Shubham with enough inspiration for his comics every day. You can check out all his comics on Instagram at @corporatcomics.

CORPORAT

HOW CORPORAT ARE YOU?

Unsure if you're one? Circle True or WTF to know.

1. I love my **Job** to bits. *True / WTF*
2. Every weekend, I just can't wait for **Monday**. *True / WTF*
3. My **Boss** is my favourite human being. *True / WTF*
4. What's my passion, you ask? **Excel Sheets**! *True / WTF*
5. **Company Values** run in my bloodstream. *True / WTF*
6. My ambition is be as inspiring as my **CEO**. *True / WTF*
7. I don't do my job for **Money**. Not at all! *True / WTF*
8. My **Team** is my best friend. *True / WTF*
9. My **Emails** are making the world a better place. *True / WTF*
10. My idea of fun is our monthly office **Townhall**. *True / WTF*

The number of WTFs multiplied by 10 is how Corporat you are (out of 100), e.g. 7 WTFs = 70% Corporat.

No WTFs? You're so Corporatized that you can't even see how miserable you are. Hope that denial is helping you get by.

Why 'Monday to Friday'?

For what else is Corporat life but finding survival hacks to get through Monday to Friday.

This book is a collection of the comics I have published over the years about different days and what they have come to mean to us. Find solace in the fact that you're not alone - in your suffering on a Monday, or in your struggle to get through the week, even in your celebration of the much awaited weekend.

PS: Of course, not everyone has just a 5-day work week - if you're not that 'lucky', my condolences.

To my wife Navia, the OG Corporat.

And to my family.

And to my family at work.
Remember, we're not colleagues, we are family?

INDEX

MONDAY

"What's in a name? That which we call a Monday by any other name would suck as bad.

- William Shakespeare

We love to hate Mondays

What's there to like anyway? Right after the two days of the weekend, where you realise life is more than perpetual deadlines and never-ending meetings, Monday comes knocking at your door ready to take all the hate. Monday becomes the target of all our loathing - for work in general, for the drudgery of 9-to-5, for our bosses, for frustrating processes in office. But doesn't ranting about Monday make us feel a little better? No wonder then, that my Monday Comics often end up being the most loved by Corporats like you.

VIBE CHECK

HOW BLUE ARE YOU THIS MONDAY?

All Mondays are blue, but some bluer than others.

Total **Meetings** you have today:	_____ *x 2*
Review catchups with **Boss** today:	_____ *x 5*
Number of **Deadlines** today:	_____ *x 10*
Did you have a **Working Weekend**?	*+10 if Yes*
Add them all up. Total so far:	_______
Multipliers	
Is it a Monday after **Holidays**?	*Multiply by 2 if Yes*
Are you **WFH** today?	*Divide by 2 if Yes*
Do you have a **Hangover**?	*Multiply by 2 if Yes*

That is how % Blue you are today. (46 implies 46% Blue)

0 to 25% - You don't get Mondays like those often. Enjoy it!
25 to 50% - A regular Monday! Rant it out and you'll be fine
50 to 100% - You totally need those extra caffeine shots today
More than 100% - Just do yourself a favour and call in sick!

CANCEL MONDAYS, SAVE HUMANITY

JUST WHEN I'M FINALLY GETTING INTO WEEKEND MOOD..
!!
MONDAY DREAD

NOT GETTING THE MONDAY FEELING YET..
ESCALATION!
REMINDER!
REMINDER!
ESCALATION!
GOT IT.

BOSS IN FOUL MOOD, EXPECT THUNDERSTORMS. FOLLOW-UP MAILS FLOODING INBOXES. ALL IN ALL, A USUAL MONDAY.
Today's Forecast

MONDAY REGRETS

WHY DID I WASTE A WEEKEND ON THAT!

WHY DID I HAVE THAT SHOT!

WHY DID I PILE THAT WORK UP!

WHY AM I DOING THIS JOB!

?

WHEN
MONDAY HASN'T
EVEN STARTED BUT
YOU'RE ALREADY
COUNTING
MINUTES TILL
ITS END..

NOT ALL MONDAYS ARE TERRIBLE.
SOME ARE JUST BAD.

WHOA! IS THAT AN EARTHQUAKE?
NOPE! JUST MONDAY.

ME ENTERING A NEW WEEK ENERGISED..
Oh no!
Sudden Monday Morning Review

I DON'T KNOW WHY PEOPLE CRIB. I ACTUALLY LOVE MONDAYS!
LOSER!
YOU PSYCHOPATH!
WHAT A CREEP!
AM I!?

monday inspiration

No search results found.

MONDAY BLUES HI

NO MONDAY BLUES TODAY..
COZ I WAS WORKING THE ENTIRE WEEKEND!

I WANT THIS OPTION EVERY MONDAY WHEN I LOG IN..

GETTING DRAGGED
OUT OF BED..
Nooooo!!
MONDAY

A NEW MEANINGLESS WEEK! WONDER WHY I DO THIS! I SHOULD START MY OWN COMPANY. I HAVE THE PERFECT NAME FOR IT - ADZILLA. I'M SO EXCITED! SHOULD I EVEN GO TO OFFICE TODAY!? NAH! SHOULD ADZILLA HAVE ONE Y OR 2...
Your office cab is here!
Sh*t! Coming in a minute.
MONDAY SHOWERS

MONDAY MORNING

WHAT IT FEELS LIKE

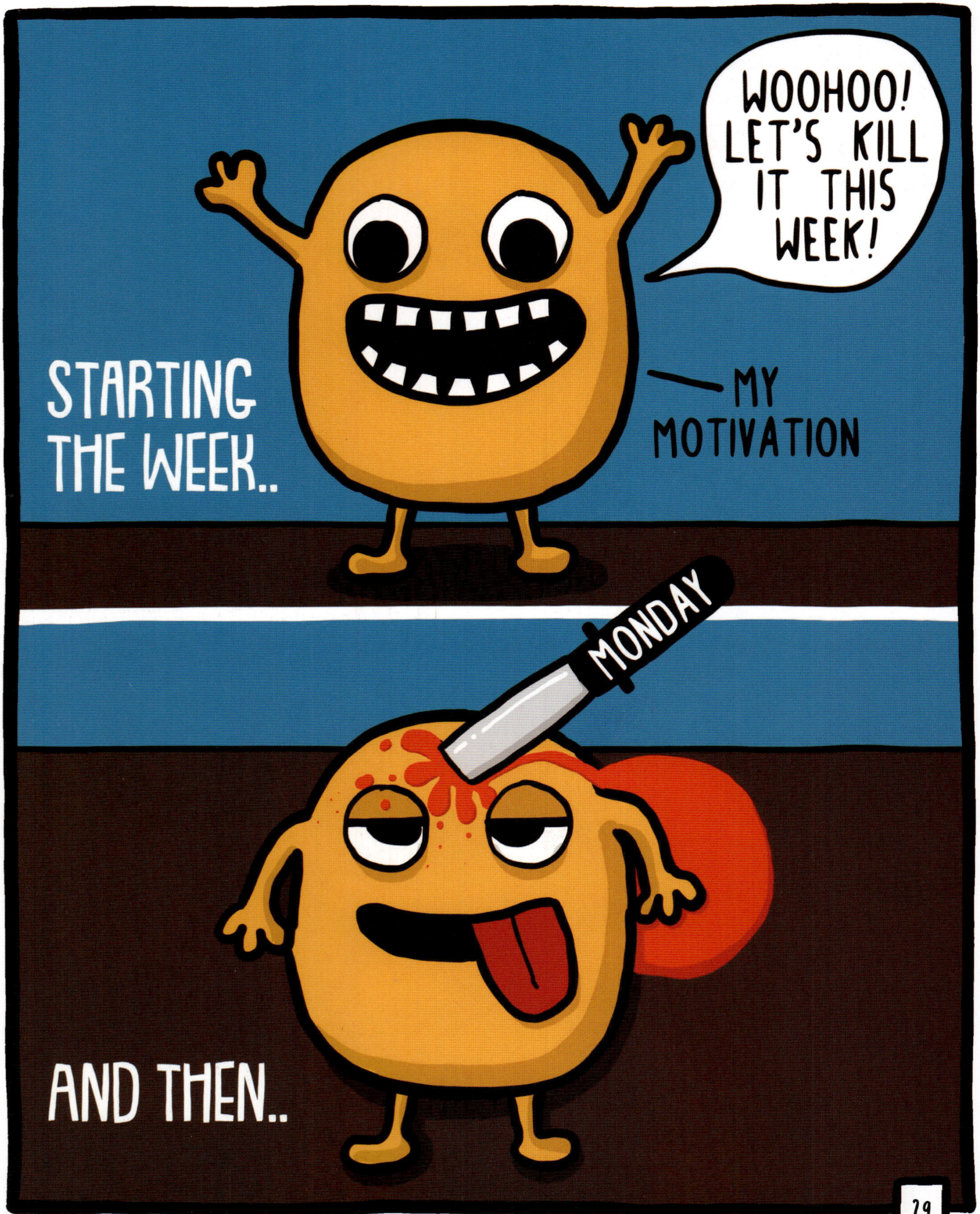

STARTING THE WEEK..

WOOHOO! LET'S KILL IT THIS WEEK!

MY MOTIVATION

WALKING INTO THE WEEK ON A MONDAY MORNING..

THE ONE THING I NEED ON MONDAY..
REWIND TO LAST WEEKEND
FORWARD TO NEXT WEEKEND

OPENING LAPTOP ON MONDAY
PENDING MAILS, TASKS

PROTEST AGAINST HATE
ALL DAYS ARE EQUAL
ALL DAYS MATTER
MON
26
19
MON
12
3
MONDAYS HAVE FEELINGS TOO.

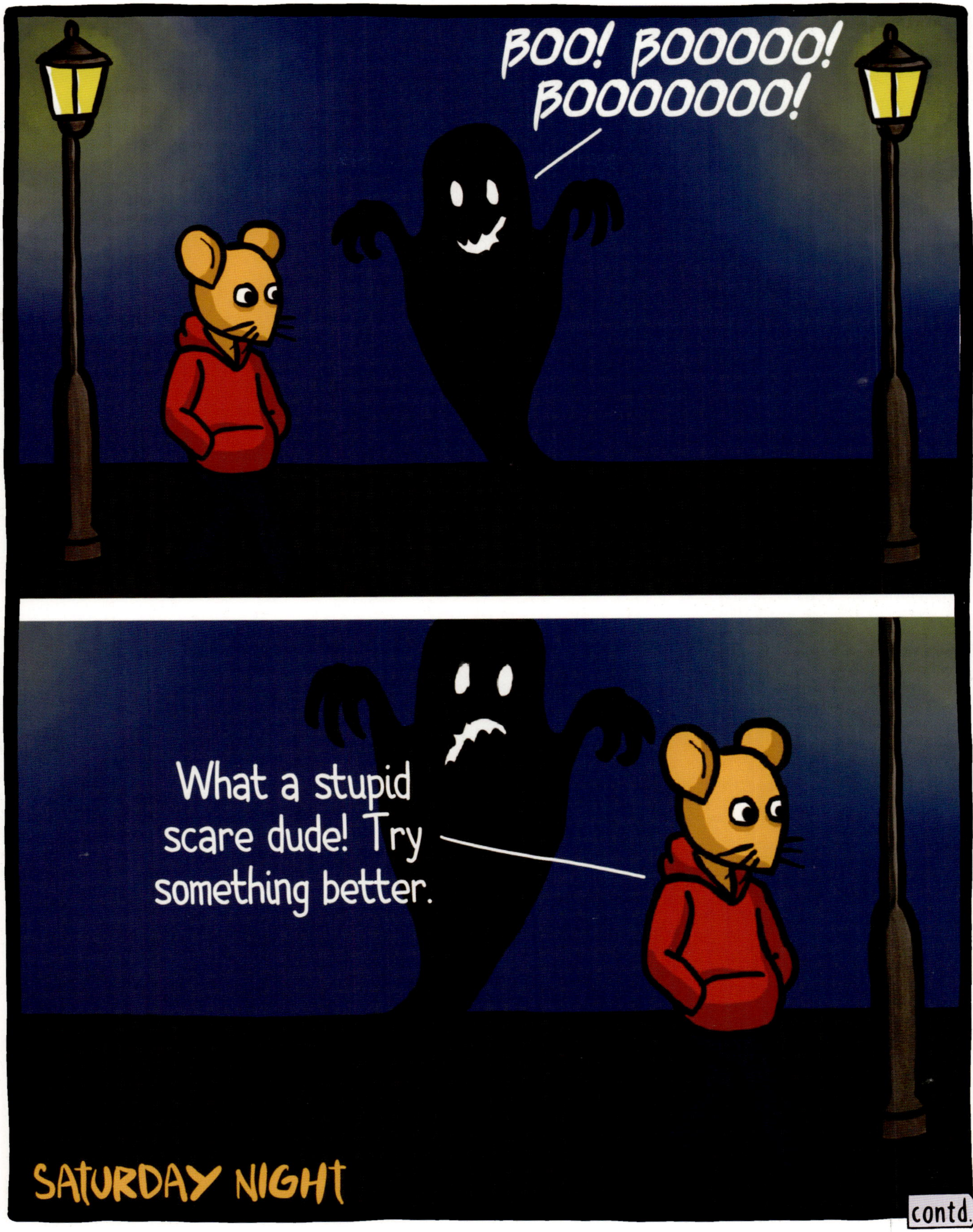

BOO! BOOOOO! BOOOOOOO!

SATURDAY NIGHT

contd.

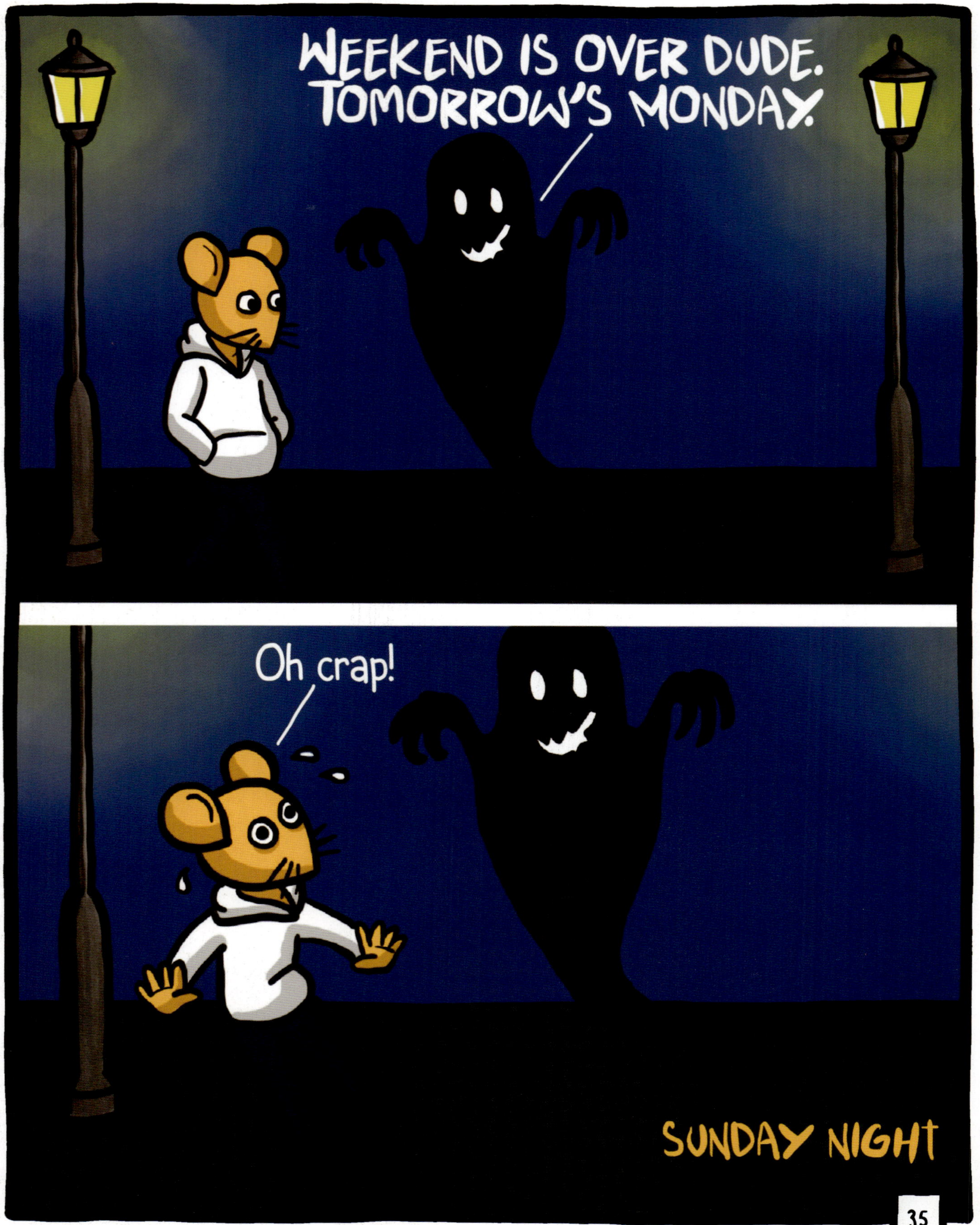

WEEKEND IS OVER DUDE. TOMORROW'S MONDAY.

COFFEE

"The way to get started is to quit talking and begin caffeinating.

- Walt Disney

Coffee, the elixir of life

If Monday is the real villain, then Coffee is the knight in shining armour. Imagine going over your excel sheets without having your cup of coffee. Or a morning review without one! Now throw Monday into the mix! Scared? Scarred? I won't blame you. Coffee makes everything better - even Mondays. Or chai, if that's your poison.

DECISIONS

SHOULD YOU HAVE ANOTHER COFFEE?

Connect the dots to find the answer.

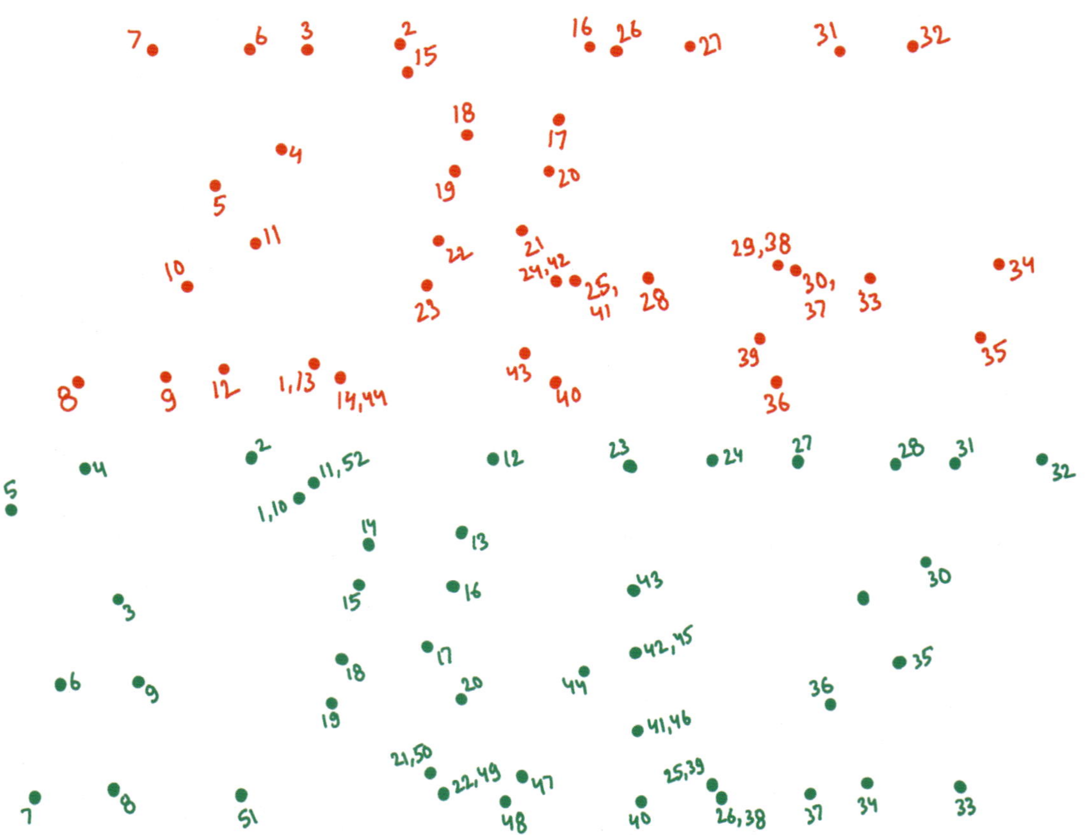

MY BIGGEST NIGHTMARE: IT'S MONDAY AND I'M OUT OF COFFEE

MONDAY

31

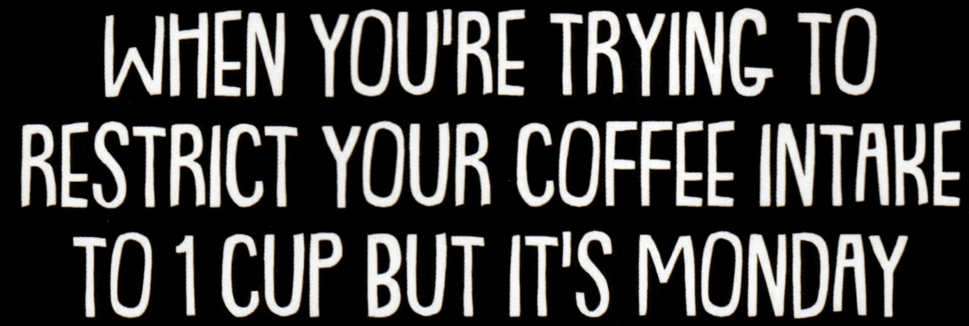
WHEN YOU'RE TRYING TO
RESTRICT YOUR COFFEE INTAKE
TO 1 CUP BUT IT'S MONDAY

COFFEE
K.O.
MONDAY

MON

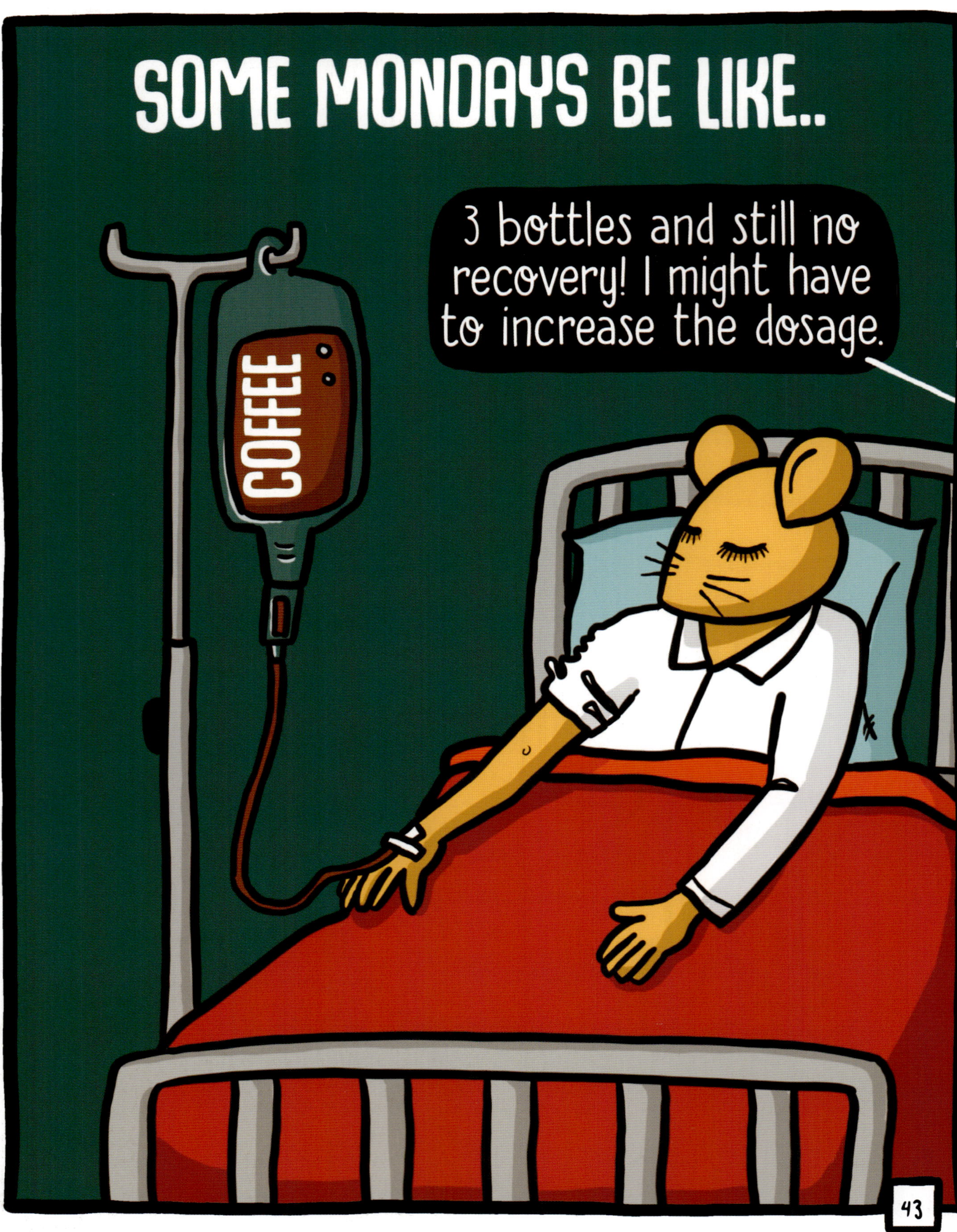
SOME MONDAYS BE LIKE..
3 bottles and still no recovery! I might have to increase the dosage.
COFFEE

ME BEFORE COFFEE ON MONDAY

ME AFTER ONE CUP

ME AFTER THREE CUPS

Short

Tall

Grande

Monday

Corporat Cafe

MONDAY AFTER A LONG WEEKEND
COFFEE

MONDAY MORNING RITUAL
COFFEE

MAKING COFFEE
MAKING COFFEE ON A MONDAY
MAKING COFFEE ON A MONDAY WHEN BOSS PINGS YOU FOR AN URGENT 1:1 CATCH-UP

SOME MONDAYS, YOU NEED MUCH MORE THAN JUST A CUP OF COFFEE

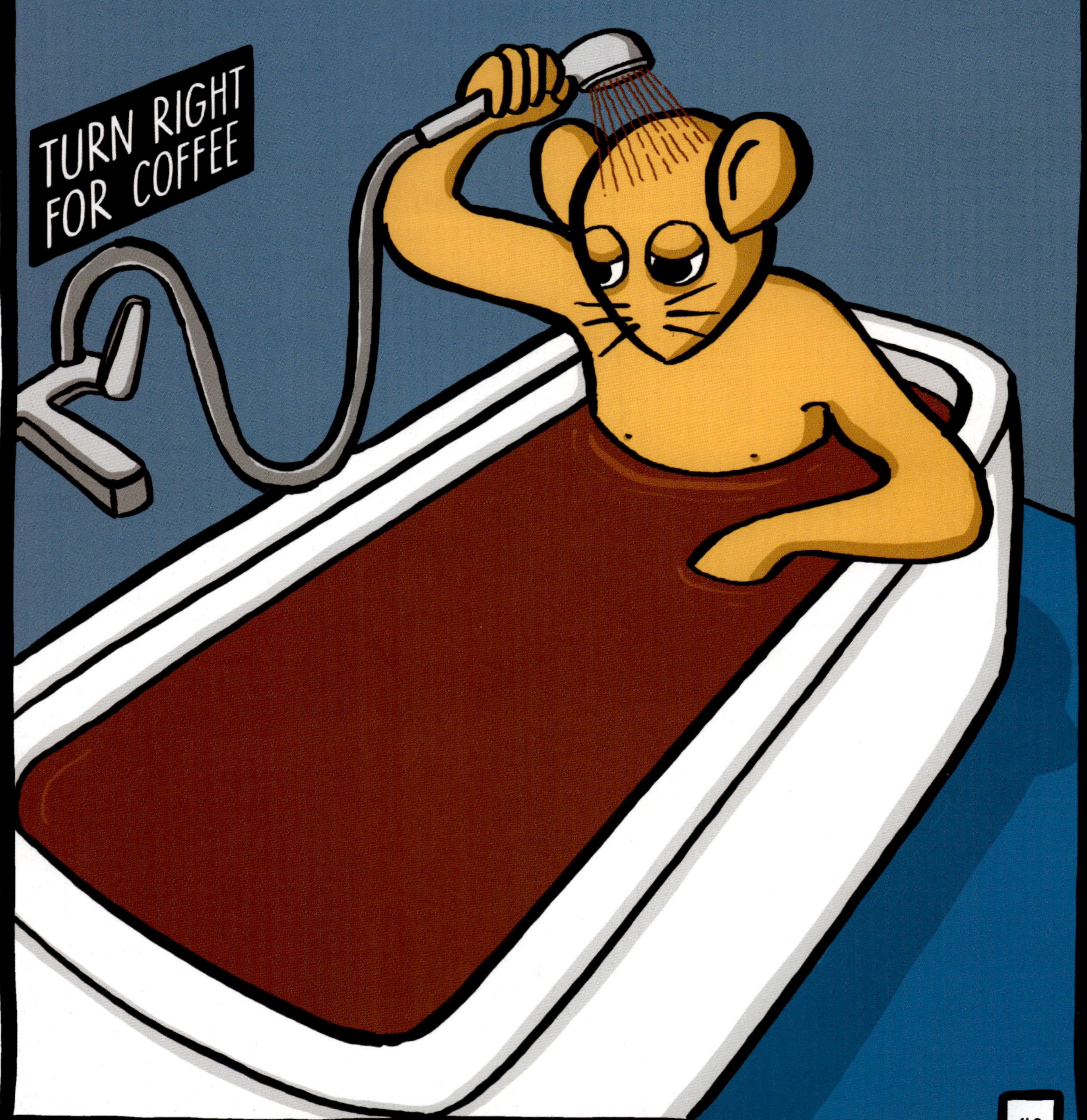

MID WEEK

"It is during our darkest days that we must focus to see the weekend

- Aristotle

Why only hate on one day?

Tuesday is as much of a pain in the ass as Monday is. There, someone had to say it! Wednesday is even worse. And Thursday, don't even get me started. While the first day of the week ends up getting all the hate, the other days deserve your hate too. Go on then, let's hate on all of them.

THE WORST

WHICH DAY IS THE ABSOLUTE WORST?

Circle the days to find your answer.

1. I get the most **work requests** on	*Tue / Wed / Thu*
2. My **office parties** rarely happen on	*Tue / Wed / Thu*
3. I can never **work from home** on	*Tue / Wed / Thu*
4. This week's **calendar** is most packed on	*Tue / Wed / Thu*
5. My **boss** calls me the most on	*Tue / Wed / Thu*
6. By this day, I've had enough of my **team**	*Tue / Wed / Thu*
7. The worst **traffic** is always on	*Tue / Wed / Thu*
8. I start counting hours to the **weekend** on	*Tue / Wed / Thu*
9. I took the most **chai-coffee breaks** on	*Tue / Wed / Thu*

Now just add the scores for each. See, Monday just gets all the hate but there are other days which are as bad (or worse).

PS: If you could not think beyond Monday for all of these, congrats, you don't hate your job. You just hate Mondays.

SOME TUESDAYS BE LIKE..

IS IT FRIDAY YET?

I'm the scariest!
People hate no one
one more than me!
Challenge accepted!
MONDAY
TUESDAY

SOME DAYS,
I WISH MY
KEYBOARD
HAD THIS
BUTTON!

GET ME
OUT OF
HERE !!

ESC
F1
F2
~
1
2
3
TAB
Q
W
E
CAPS
A
S
D
Z
X
C
CTRL
SPACE

OH LOOK, A FORTUNE COOKIE! LET'S SEE WHAT IT SAYS ABOUT THE COMING WEEK.

Oops!

TUESDAY IS JUST ANOTHER MONDAY WITH A MASK ON

THE ONE DAY I PLAN TO LEAVE OFFICE EARLY
People who want to speak to me 'for 2 mins' just when I'm stepping out

THAT CONFUSING FEELING ON THURSDAY EVE WHEN IT SEEMS THE WEEK IS OVER BUT WEEKEND IS ACTUALLY A DAY AWAY

YAY IT'S FRIDAY TOMORROW !!

MEANWHILE THURSDAY

ME ON THURSDAY..
TODAY'S FRIDAY, RIGHT?
RIGHT!?

SOME MORNINGS, IT'S HARD TO CHOOSE WHAT WOULD HELP ME GET THROUGH MY WORK DAY..
COFFEE

I SPENT SO MUCH TIME RANTING ABOUT MONDAY BLUES YESTERDAY..
contd.

I ENDED UP DOING HARDLY ANY WORK..
Task
AND IT KEPT PILING..
Task
Task
Task
contd.

TO THE EXTENT THAT..

Task

Task

Task

Task

Task

contd.

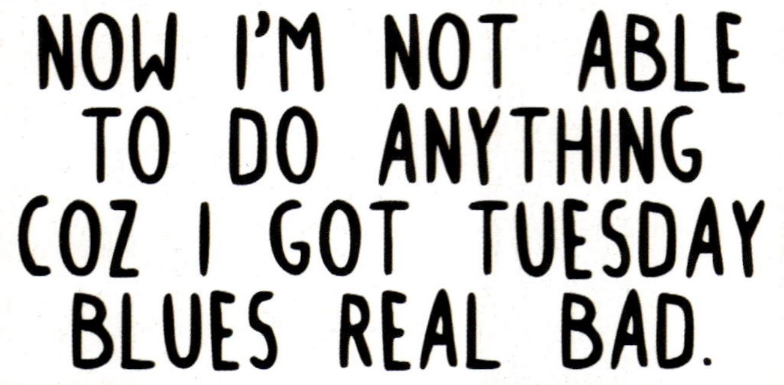
NOW I'M NOT ABLE TO DO ANYTHING COZ I GOT TUESDAY BLUES REAL BAD.

FRIDAY

"Leave nothing for Friday which can be done next week.

- Abraham Lincoln

There's a Yay in Friday

You've felt it! The first whiff of the Friday air brings with it the feeling that the long dreaded week is finally over. Postpone those meetings, ignore those deadlines, don't even open those emails. They can all wait, they're not meant for Fridays, the sender should know better. If my Monday comics are morose, no surprises that the Friday ones are equally cheerful. After all, the day holds in itself, the promise of a not-so-sober evening and the weekend thereafter.

YAY OR NAY

WILL THIS BE A FRIYAY OR FRINAY?

Select True or False to find out.

1. My **boss** is not coming to office this Friday *True / False*
2. I don't have a lot of **pending tasks** this Friday *True / False*
3. My team is stepping out for **drinks** this Friday *True / False*
4. I'm 'working' (lol) from **home** this Friday *True / False*
5. I'm on **leave / holiday** this Friday *True / False*
6. My Friday **review** got shifted to next week *True / False*
7. We have a **celebration** at office this Friday *True / False*
8. My **calendar** looks quite chill this Friday *True / False*
9. I have no **deadlines** falling on Friday *True / False*

More True? Thank God it's FriYay!

More False? Cancel those meetings. Ignore those deadlines. Make a plan with your team and rant your heart out. Making it a FriYay is your responsibility.

WEEKEND
ME
THAT COLLEAGUE WHO COMES WITH A LAST MINUTE WORK REQUEST ON FRIDAY

EVEN SHITTY OFFICE COFFEE
TASTES GREAT ON A FRIDAY

ME DESPERATELY
WAITING FOR
BOSS TO LEAVE
OFFICE ON FRIDAY
SO I CAN START
MY WEEKEND

FRIYAY
CAN WE TALK?
FRIYAY
BOSS

CONGRATULATIONS! YOU'VE COMPLETED ANOTHER WEEK OF BEING INSIGNIFICANT.
THE REAL FRIDAY FEELING..

FRIDAY-ME
MONDAY-ME WILL TAKE CARE OF IT
WORK
contd.

MONDAY-ME
A**HOLE
WORK
WORK
WORK
WORK
WORK

ME ON FRIDAY

IT'S NOT FRIDAY. IT'S I'VE-HAD-SUCH-A-LONG-WEEK-I'M-FRIED-DAY!

WONDER WHY I'M NOT GETTING THAT FRIDAY FEELING YET..

WORK
FRIDAY
RECIPE FOR DISASTER

SOME FRIDAYS, THE WEEKEND SEEMS SO CLOSE YET SO FAR..

WEATHER FEELS SO NICE

I CAN HEAR BIRDS CHIRPING

WHY IS THIS NOT IRRITATING ME
BOSS

GOT TO BE THE FRIDAY FEELING!
FRIDAY
11

FRIDAY
MOOD*
WINE
COFFEE
*NOT
RECOMMENDED
BEFORE REVIEW
MEETINGS

FRIDAY EVENING..
HEY, CAN I TAKE 2 MINS? IT'S URGENT.
1 HOUR LATER..
..AND ONE LAST QUESTION..

ME
PENDING
WORK
EMAILS
EVERY FRIDAY EVENING..

ME TO MYSELF, ON A RARE FRIDAY WHEN I FINISH ALL MY WEEK'S WORK BY 6PM..

FRIDAY RITUAL

WEEKEND

"Weekend is what happens when you're busy making annual plans.

- John Lennon

When does the week end?

5 days of work to get only 2 days off. Isn't that ironic? Wait! Are you even getting your two full days of weekend, with bosses and clients waiting like vultures to steal those precious hours with their 'urgent' work requests? The very hours you had reserved for bingeing the newest cringe show while munching on previous night's pizza - you inseparable from your couch, while you ignore the chores you had planned. Sigh! Petition to let weekends be weekends.

DILEMMA

SHOULD I PICK BOSS'S WEEKEND CALL?

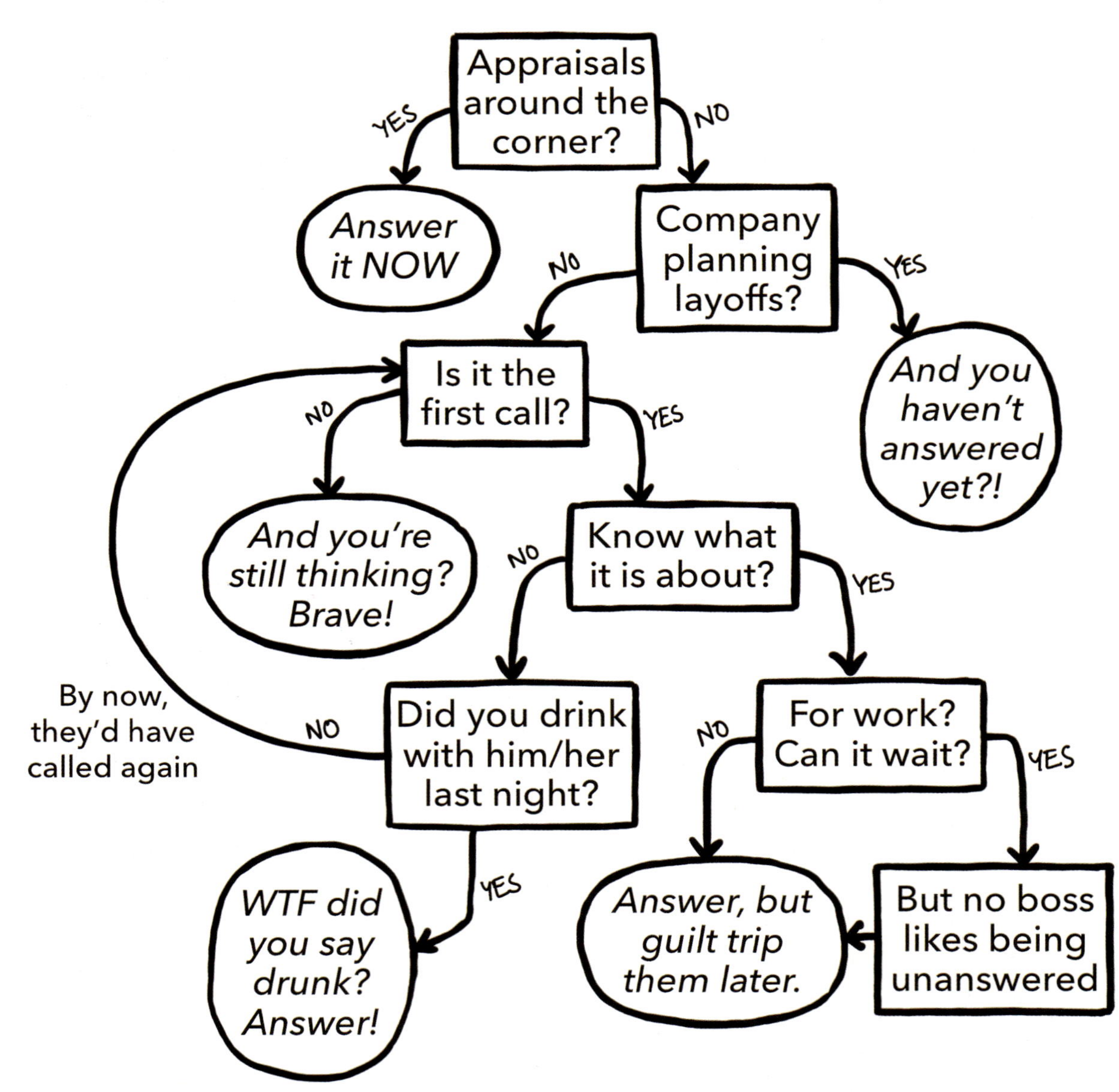

I'M STILL REGRETTING WASTING LAST WEEKEND ON A CRAPPY SHOW.
PLANS FOR THIS WEEKEND? THE SAME.

WHAT A LONG WEEK! GLAD IT'S OVEE..
PING!!
..ERRR!!??
Urgent work! Finish it by Monday 8am.

AM I THE ONLY ONE WAITING FOR THE WEEKEND BEFORE THE WEEK HAS EVEN STARTED?

DOESN'T FEEL MUCH LIKE A WEEKEND WHEN HALF OF THE WEEK WAS OFF.
BOSS:
Urgent work! Need to finish by Monday.
NOW IT DOES.

WORK
WHEN BOSS SAYS
SOME WORK
MIGHT SPILL OVER
INTO THE WEEKEND

AND IN TODAY'S EPISODE OF WEEKEND FORECAST WITH BOSS..

ME TRYING TO GET SMASHED BEFORE MONDAY DREAD HITS
Shots!!
Shots!
QUICKLY! I FEEL IT COMING..
PARTY ANIMAL

ME TRYING
TO CHILL
OVER THE
WEEKEND
RESPONSIBILITIES
EXISTENCE
MONDAY DREAD
PLANS
CHORES
WOR

WEEKEND OPTIONS

CHILLING

DREADING NEXT WEEK

ME EVERY WEEKEND

TIME TO DO THE CHORES I COULDN'T DURING THE WEEK.
NAH! WEEKEND IS FOR DOING NOTHING.

WOW! IT'S LIKE THE CLOUDS ARE TRYING TO TELL ME SOMETHING.
tomorrow's monday
WTF!

Weekend Plans..

contd.

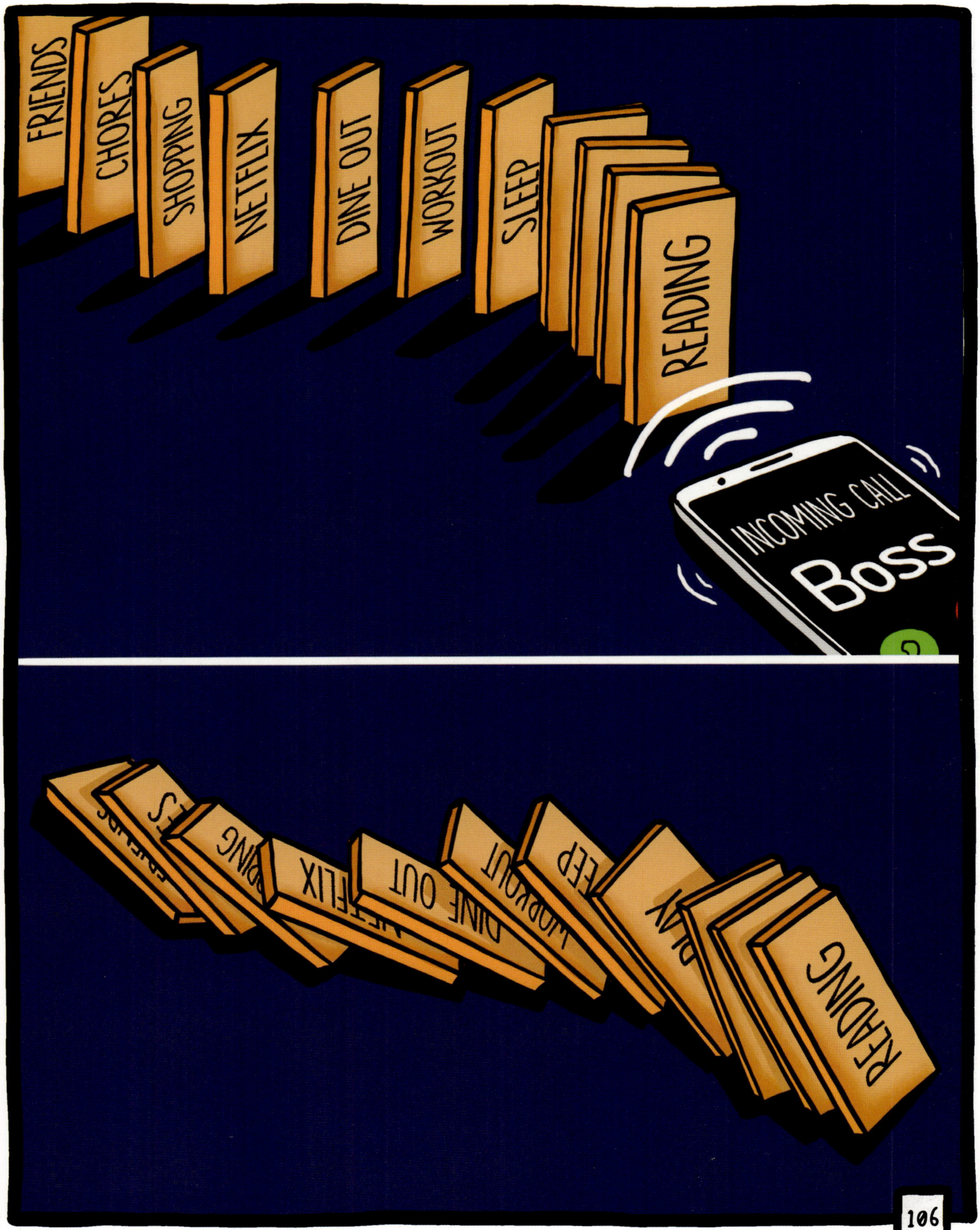

FRIENDS
CHORES
SHOPPING
NETFLIX
DINE OUT
WORKOUT
SLEEP
READING
INCOMING CALL
Boss

HOLIDAYS

"You miss 100%
of the leaves you
don't take.

- Wayne Gretzky

When's the long weekend?

I'm sure you know. A true Corporat always keeps a track. In my opinion, all weekends should be long weekends, but who's listening! Have you wondered how we don't call a five-day week 'long week', but we end up calling a three-day weekend 'long weekend'? Ironic! But rant aside, nothing is more precious to us Corporats than those holidays, providing us that temporary escape from work. But do they really?

CHECKLIST

PREPARING TO ASK FOR A LEAVE

You sure you're ready? Check these to find out.

[ ] Been **'seen' slogging** my ass off this month

[ ] Brought **homemade biryani** for boss last week

[ ] Took only half the usual **coffee breaks** this week

[ ] Was the first to LOL at **boss's jokes** in our WhatsApp group

[ ] Asked for 'additional responsibilities' to **contribute** more

[ ] Was always **typing furiously** when boss walked past me

[ ] Used terms like **'accountability'** and **'agility'** in meetings

[ ] Researched to confirm all is well in boss's **personal life**

[ ] Unequivocally supported all new **org initiatives** lately

[ ] Verified with HR that there are **no layoffs** being planned

Something left unchecked? You aren't ready yet!
Spend another week ticking off all this and try again.

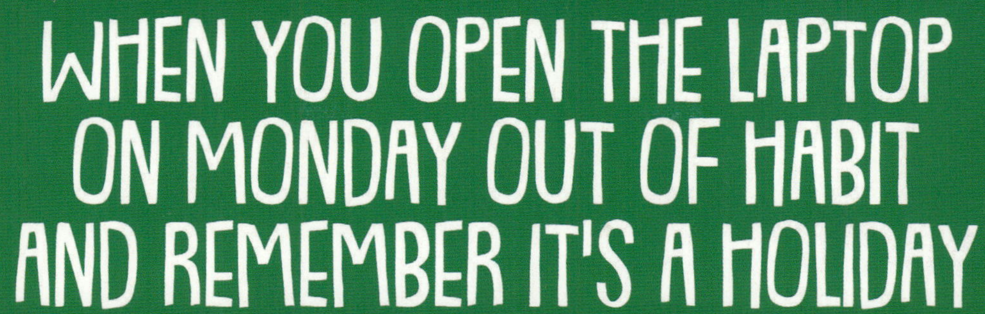
WHEN YOU OPEN THE LAPTOP
ON MONDAY OUT OF HABIT
AND REMEMBER IT'S A HOLIDAY
TEARS OF JOY

NOTHING HURTS MORE THAN REALISING YOUR FRIENDS HAVE A HOLIDAY ON MONDAY BUT YOU DON'T

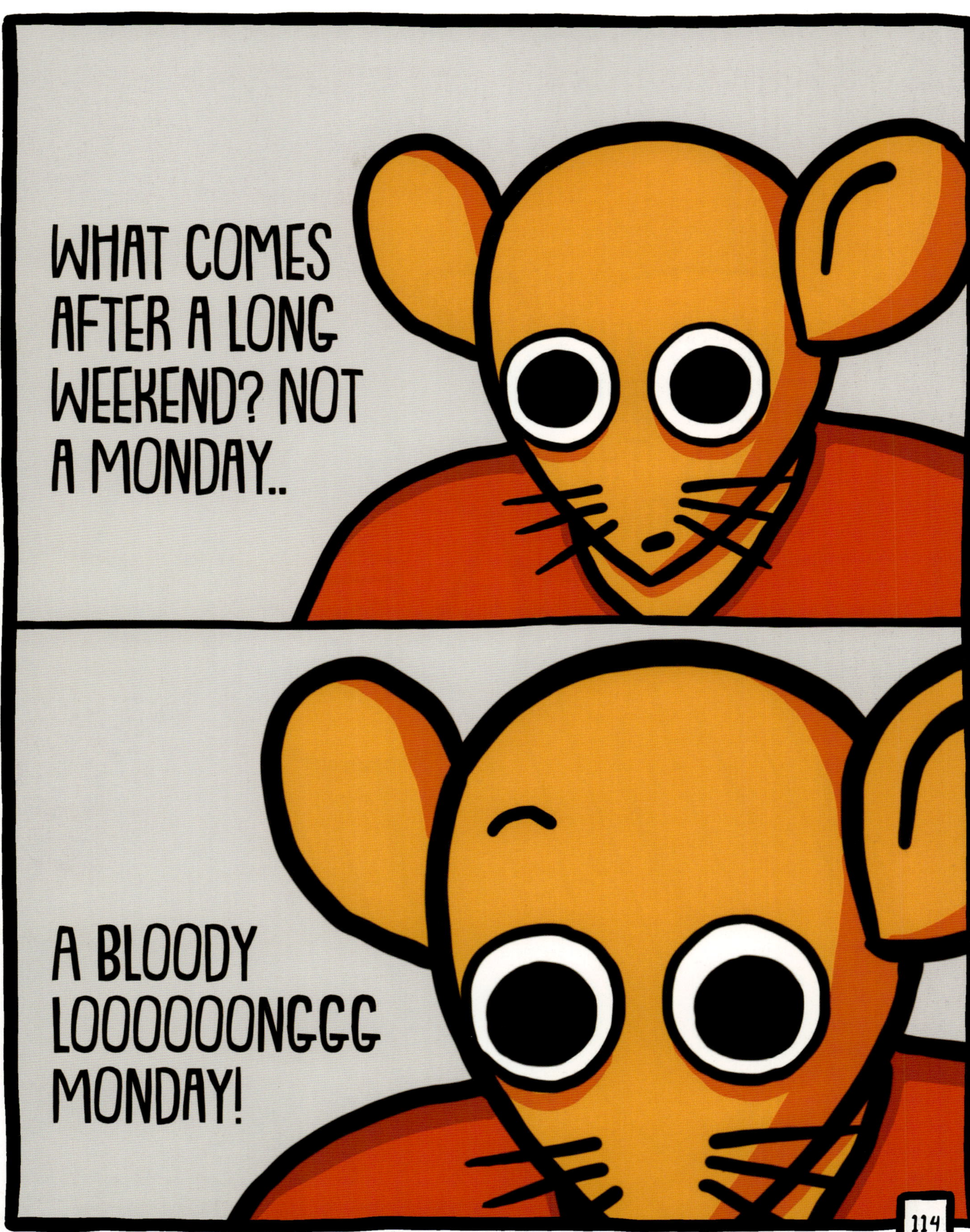
WHAT COMES AFTER A LONG WEEKEND? NOT A MONDAY..
A BLOODY LOOOOOOONGGG MONDAY!

WHEN YOU HATE WEDNESDAYS BUT THIS THURSDAY IS A HOLIDAY
TO CRIB OR NOT TO CRIB, THAT IS THE QUESTION.

SAW HIS INSTA PICS? HOW DID HE GET 2 WEEKS OFF WHILE I DIDN'T!
SHH.. LET ME AT LEAST RANT IN PEACE.
BUT YOU TOOK LEAVES IN APRI..

WHEN MOST OF YOUR TEAM IS ON LEAVE BECAUSE THEY'RE NOT WELL, AND YOU FEEL BAD ABOUT BEING TOTALLY HEALTHY

IF TODAY IS 'LABOUR' DAY, WHAT'S REST OF THE YEAR?

NO, IT ISN'T ANOTHER WAVE. THE ENTIRE TEAM INCIDENTALLY ALWAYS FALLS UNWELL ON MONDAYS WHEN TUESDAYS ARE OFF!

ICEBERGS ARE MELTING! WE'RE HEADED TOWARDS A CATASTROPHE! PENGUINS AND ALL.. WHALES.. FUEL.. WATER.. OZONE LAYER.. THEN WHY ISN'T IT A HOLIDAY!?
Save Our P
CORPORATS, REALISING IT'S EARTH DAY

THE LONG-WEEKEND CONSPIRACY

IS IT NORMAL TO GET MONDAY BLUES ON A THURSDAY JUST AFTER A MID-WEEK HOLIDAY?

OUT-OF-OFFICE
OUT-OF-OFFICE
OUT-OF-OFFICE
OUT-OF-OFFICE
WHAT IT LOOKS LIKE
YOU LOSER!!
YOU LOSER!!
YOU LOSER!!
YOU LOSER!!
WHAT IT FEELS LIKE

ME, THE MONDAY
AFTER HOLIDAY WEEK,
HAVING SHIFTED ALL
MY MEETINGS TO
"EARLY NEXT WEEK"

WHEN YOU'RE BORED AT WORK BUT CAN'T EVEN INSTAGRAM COZ IT'S FILLED WITH FRIENDS' VACAY PICS MAKING YOU FEEL WORSE

ENTERING
LONG
WEEKEND
Woohoo!
contd.

MONDAY
AFTER THE
LONG
WEEKEND
Oops!

OUT OF OFFICE EMAILS

WHAT I SAY..

I'm out of office and will be back next week.

WHAT I WANT TO SAY..

SCREW YOU SLAVE COZ I'LL BE SIPPING MARTINIS BY THE BEACH WHILE YOU SLOG!

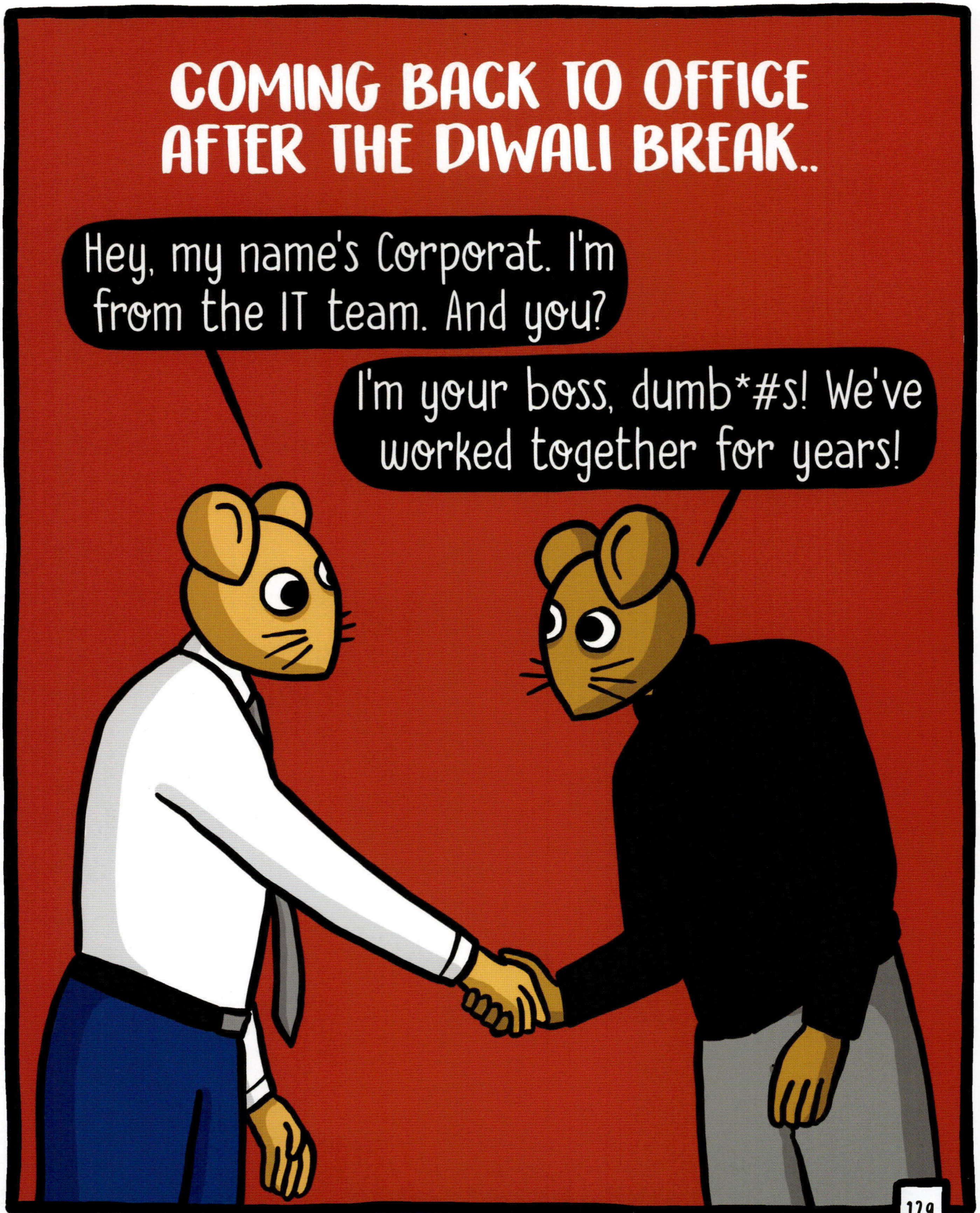

COMING BACK TO OFFICE AFTER THE DIWALI BREAK..

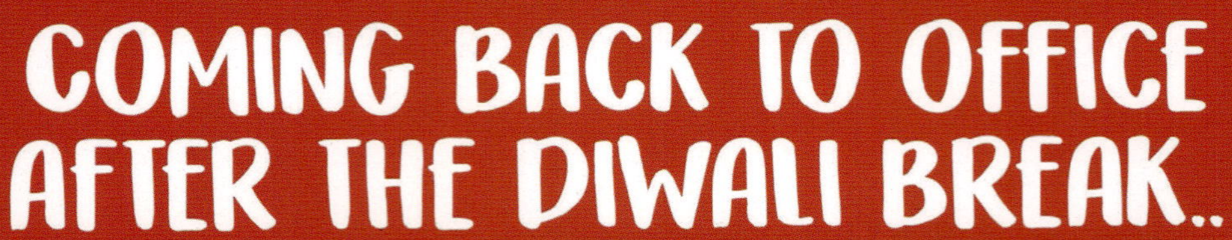

THE MONDAY AFTER A LONG WEEKEND
Coffee

WOOHOO! NO MONDAY THIS WEEK..

WHAACKK!!

TUESDAY

LOOKING AT MY LAPTOP AFTER THE LONG WEEKEND
Wow! So many buttons! What is this device? A spaceship?

PENDING WORK BEFORE GOING FOR VACATION
PENDING WORK WHEN I COME BACK

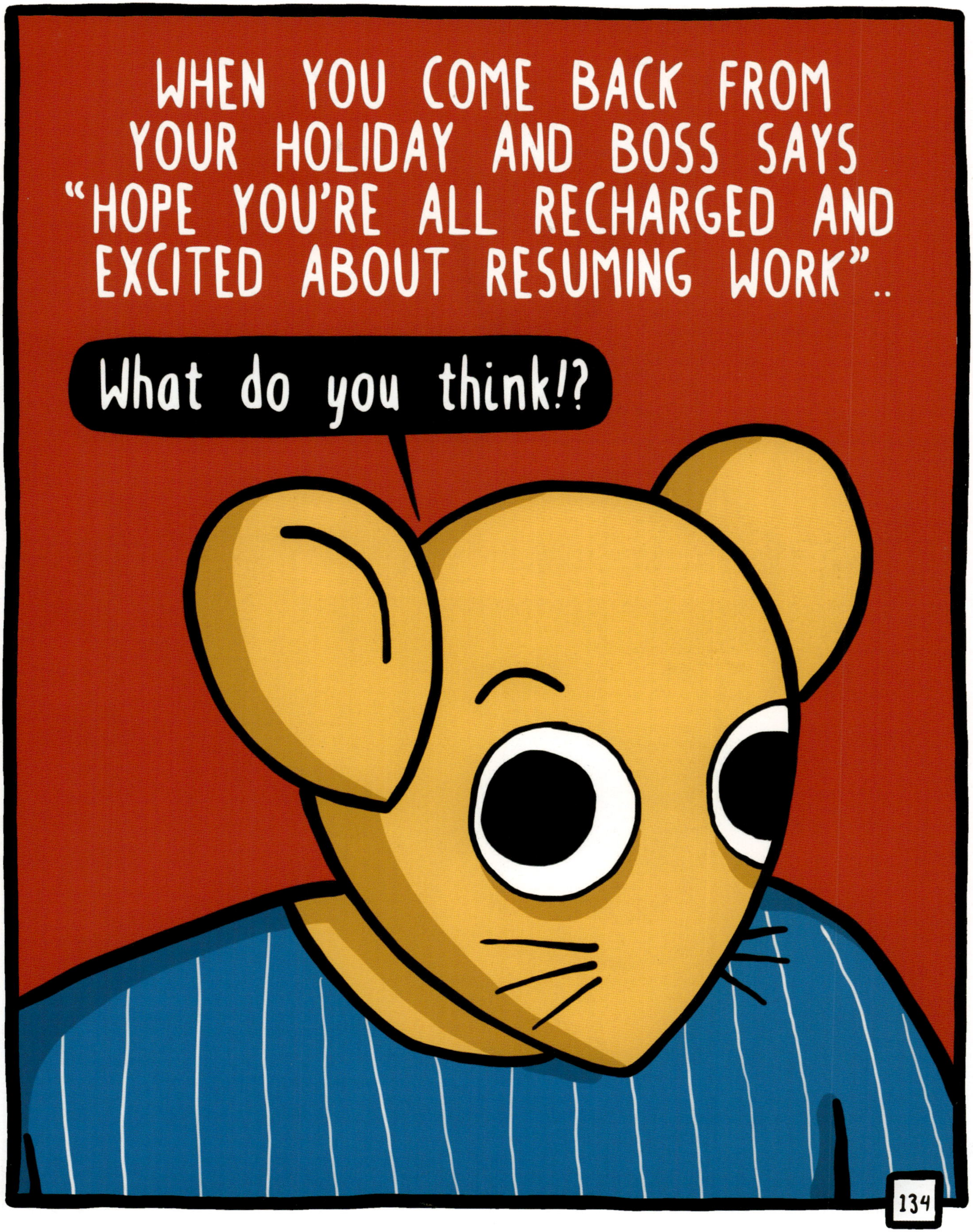

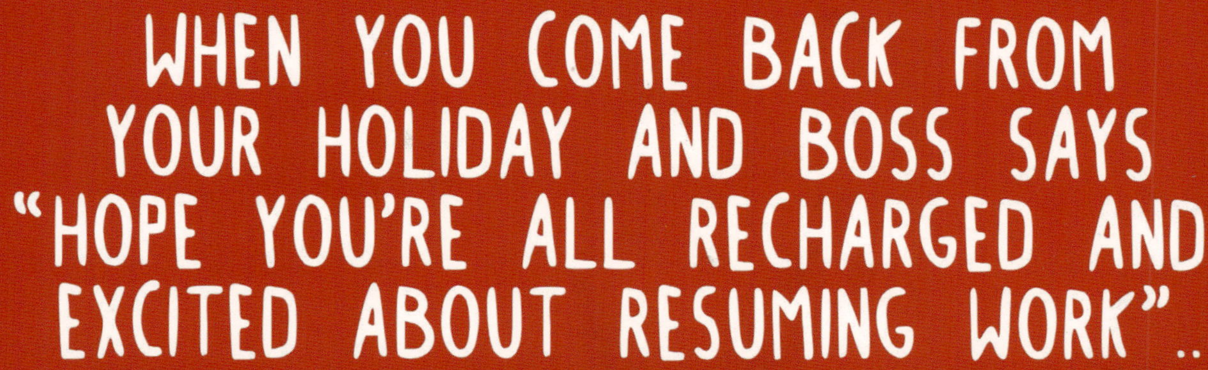
WHEN YOU COME BACK FROM YOUR HOLIDAY AND BOSS SAYS "HOPE YOU'RE ALL RECHARGED AND EXCITED ABOUT RESUMING WORK"..
What do you think!?

MONDAY
LAST MONDAY OF THE YEAR WHEN YOU CAN CHILL AS EVERYONE INCLUDING BOSS IS ON LEAVE

I TRIED WITH ALL MY STRENGTH, BUT JUST COULDN'T GET HIM TO WORK.
THESE POST-HOLIDAY BLUES ARE UNBEATABLE!

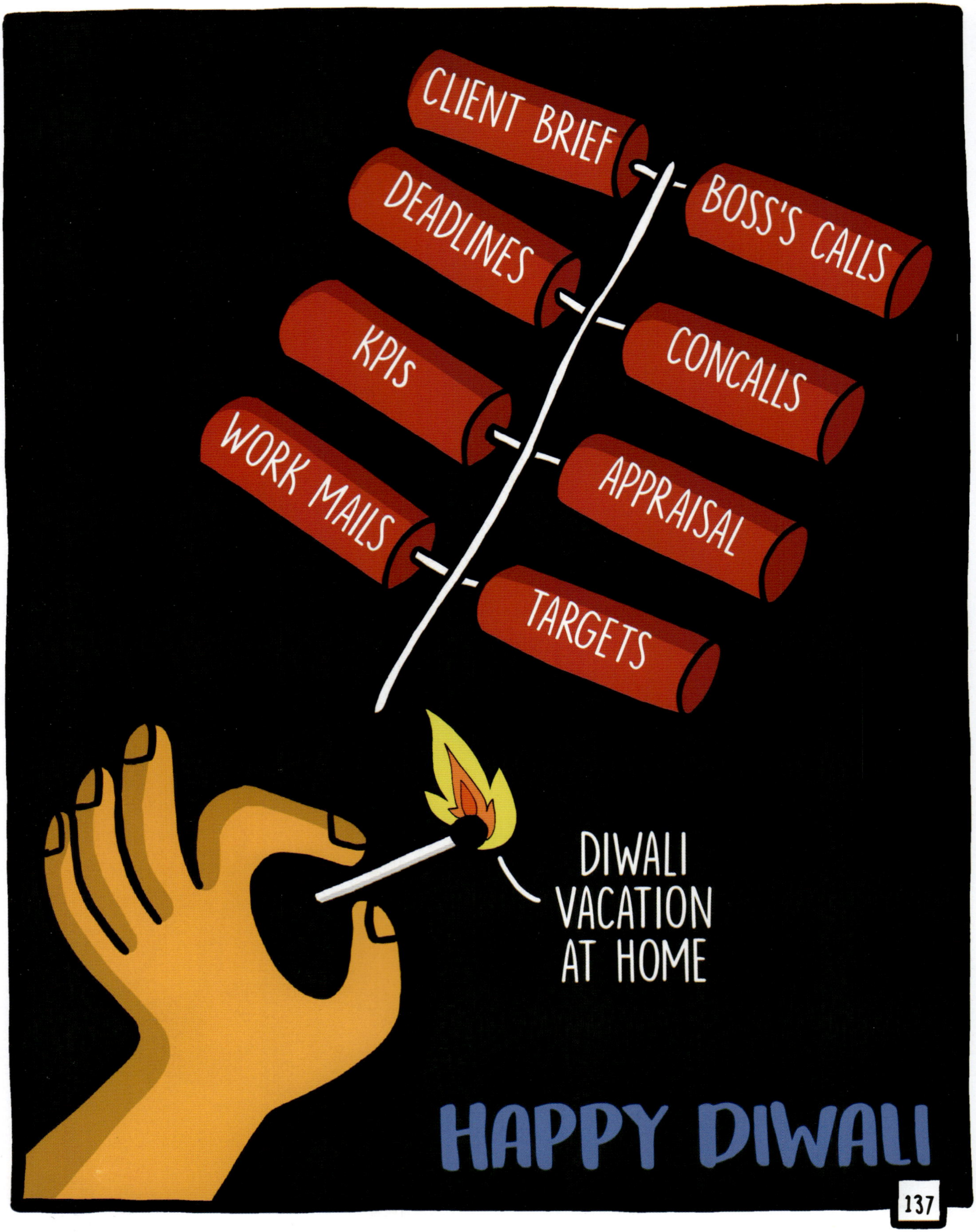

CLIENT BRIEF
BOSS'S CALLS
DEADLINES
CONCALLS
KPIs
APPRAISAL
WORK MAILS
TARGETS

DIWALI
VACATION
AT HOME

HAPPY DIWALI

Existence is meaningless.
WHEN YOU REALISE THE LAST LONG WEEKEND OF THE YEAR IS OVER